SCHOLASTIC

READ & RESPOND

Helping children discover the pleasure and power of reading

THE GIRL WHO STOLE an ELEPHANT

"Adventuring at its best"
Gill Lewis

NIZRANA FAROOK

nosy crow

FOR AGES 9–11

Published in the UK by Scholastic Education, 2022
Scholastic Distribution Centre, Bosworth Avenue, Tournament Fields, Warwick, CV34 6UQ
Scholastic Ireland, 89E Lagan Road, Dublin Industrial Estate, Glasnevin, Dublin, D11 HP5F

1 2 3 4 5 6 7 8 9   2 3 4 5 6 7 8 9 0 1
Printed and bound by Ashford Colour Press

The book is made of materials from well-managed,
FSC®-certified forests and other controlled sources.

A CIP catalogue record for this book is available from the British Library.
ISBN 978-0702-31946-4

Printed and bound by Ashford Colour Press
Paper made from wood grown in sustainable forests and other controlled sources.

Extracts from *The National Curriculum in England, English Programme of Study* © Crown Copyright. Reproduced under the terms of the Open Government Licence (OGL). http://www.nationalarchives.gov.uk/doc/open-government-licence/version/3

Authors Sally Burt and Debbie Ridgard
Editorial team Rachel Morgan, Vicki Yates, Suzanne Adams and Julia Roberts
Series designer Andrea Lewis
Typesetter QBS Learning
Illustrator Juanita Londono
Photographs page 18: Train from Kandy to Ella, Creative Family/Shutterstock

Acknowledgements
The publishers gratefully acknowledge permission to reproduce the following material:
Nosy Crow Ltd for the use of the text extracts and cover from *The Girl Who Stole an Elephant* by Nizrana Farook. Text © 2020.

Every effort has been made to trace copyright holders for the works reproduced in this book, and the publishers apologise for any inadvertent omissions.

For supporting online resources go to:
www.scholastic.co.uk/read-and-respond/books/girl-who-stole-an-elephant/online-resources
Access key: Model

CONTENTS ▽

How to use Read & Respond in your classroom...

Read & Respond provides teaching ideas related to a specific well-loved children's book. Each Read & Respond book is divided into the following sections:

ABOUT THE BOOK AND AUTHOR

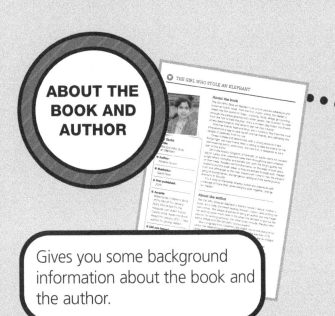

Gives you some background information about the book and the author.

GUIDED READING

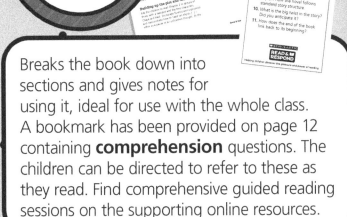

Breaks the book down into sections and gives notes for using it, ideal for use with the whole class. A bookmark has been provided on page 12 containing **comprehension** questions. The children can be directed to refer to these as they read. Find comprehensive guided reading sessions on the supporting online resources.

SHARED READING

Provides extracts from the children's book with associated notes for focused work. There is also one non-fiction extract that relates to the children's book.

GRAMMAR, PUNCTUATION & SPELLING

Provides word-level work related to the children's book so you can teach grammar, punctuation, spelling and **vocabulary** in context.

PLOT, CHARACTER & SETTING

Contains activity ideas focused on the plot, characters and the setting of the story.

TALK ABOUT IT

Oracy, **fluency**, and speaking and listening activities. These activities may be based directly on the children's book or be broadly based on the themes and concepts of the story.

GET WRITING

Provides writing activities related to the children's book. These activities may be based directly on the children's book or be broadly based on the themes and concepts of the story.

ASSESSMENT

Contains short activities that will help you assess whether the children have understood concepts and curriculum objectives. They are designed to be informal activities to feed into your planning.

SUPPORTING ONLINE RESOURCE

Online you can find a host of supporting documents including planning information, comprehensive guided reading sessions and guidance on teaching reading.

www.scholastic.co.uk/read-and-respond/books/girl-who-stole-an-elephant/online-resources
Access key: Model

Help children develop a love of **reading for pleasure.**

Activities

The activities follow the same format:

- **Objective:** the objective for the lesson. It will be based upon a curriculum objective, but will often be more specific to the focus being covered.

- **What you need:** a list of resources you need to teach the lesson, including photocopiable pages.

- **What to do:** the activity notes.

- **Differentiation:** this is provided where specific and useful differentiation advice can be given to support and/or extend the learning in the activity. Differentiation by providing additional adult support has not been included as this will be at a teacher's discretion based upon specific children's needs and ability, as well as the availability of support.

The activities are numbered for reference within each section and should move through the text sequentially – so you can use the lesson while you are reading the book. Once you have read the book, most of the activities can be used in any order you wish.

Section	Activity	Curriculum objectives
Guided reading		Comprehension: To develop positive attitudes to reading and understanding of what they read.
Shared reading	1	Comprehension: To check the book makes sense to them, discussing their understanding and exploring the meaning of words in context.
	2	Comprehension: To discuss and evaluate how authors use language, considering the impact on the reader.
	3	Comprehension: To predict what might happen from details stated and implied.
	4	Comprehension: To identify how language, structure and presentation contribute to meaning.
Grammar, punctuation and spelling	1	Vocabulary, grammar and punctuation: To use expanded noun phrases to convey complicated information concisely.
	2	Vocabulary, grammar and punctuation: To learn the grammar for Years 5–6 in Appendix 2: to understand and use ellipsis.
	3	Transcription: To distinguish between homophones.
	4	Comprehension: To discuss their understanding and explore the meaning of words in context.
	5	Vocabulary, grammar and punctuation: To use semicolons, colons or dashes to mark boundaries between independent clauses.
	6	Vocabulary, grammar and punctuation: To recognise vocabulary that is appropriate for formal speech and writing.
Plot, character and setting	1	Comprehension: To identify how language, structure and presentation contribute to meaning.
	2	Comprehension: To make comparisons within and across books (setting).
	3	Comprehension: To make comparisons within and across books (historical fiction).
	4	Comprehension: To identify how language, structure and presentation contribute to meaning.
	5	Comprehension: To draw inferences such as inferring characters' feelings, thoughts and motives from their actions and to justify inferences with evidence.
	6	Comprehension: To discuss and evaluate how authors use language, including figurative language, considering the impact on the reader.
	7	Comprehension: To identify and discuss themes in and across a wide range of writing.
	8	Comprehension: To identify and discuss conventions in and across a wide range of writing.

Section	Activity	Curriculum objectives
Talk about it	1	Spoken language: To ask relevant questions to extend their understanding and knowledge.
	2	Spoken language: To use appropriate registers for effective communication.
	3	Spoken language: To participate in debates.
	4	Spoken language: To consider and evaluate different viewpoints.
	5	Spoken language: To participate in discussions.
	6	Spoken language: To speak audibly and fluently.
Get writing	1	Composition: To use organisational and presentational devices to structure text and to guide the reader.
	2	Composition: To write narratives, considering how authors have developed characters and settings in what they have read.
	3	Composition: To integrate dialogue; to proofread for spelling and punctuation errors.
	4	Composition: To identify the audience for and purpose of the writing and select appropriate form.
	5	Composition: To select appropriate grammar and vocabulary to enhance meaning.
	6	Composition: To write narratives, describing settings, characters and atmosphere and integrating dialogue to convey character and advance the action.
Assessment	1	Comprehension: To read aloud, showing understanding through intonation, tone and volume so that the meaning is clear. Spoken language: To speak audibly and fluently.
	2	Comprehension: To understand what they read by drawing inferences and to justify inferences with evidence.
	3	Composition: To distinguish between the language of speech and writing and to choose the appropriate register.
	4	Vocabulary, grammar and punctuation: To use hyphens in writing to avoid ambiguity.
	5	Composition: To write and perform their own compositions.
	6	Composition: To précis longer passages.

Key facts

◉ **Title:**
*The Girl Who Stole
an Elephant*

◉ **Author:**
Nizrana Farook

◉ **Illustrator:**
David Dean

◉ **First published:**
2020

◉ **Awards:**
Waterstones Children's Book
of the Month for January
2020; Shortlisted for the
inaugural Joan Aiken Future
Classics prize; Awesome Book
Award for January 2021 – new
authors for young readers

◉ **Did you know?**
It took nine months to write
the first draft of the book and
over a year of editing. The
book is not (yet) translated and
is not (yet) widely available
in Sri Lanka, modern-day
Serendib. The author loved
writing the dialogue the most.

About the book

The Girl Who Stole an Elephant is an action-packed adventure and historical fiction novel. From the first chaotic scene, the reader is swept into the world of Chaya – a young, feisty, village girl running through the palace grounds with stolen jewels. Her mission? To steal from the rich to help the poor. She's a modern-day Robin Hood with a fiery determination that tends to get her into trouble!

With her friends, Neel and Nour, she is forced to flee from the cruel King and find a way to save herself and her friends, and ultimately the people of Serendib, from his rule.

Chaya is brave and determined, with a strong desire to make things right. Her loyal friend, Neel, is willing to take the blame for her well-meaning antics, while Nour, 'the new kid', is desperate to be a part of the action.

Set in the historic Kingdom of Serendib, an earlier name for modern day Sri Lanka, their adventure takes them through the leech-infested jungle where crocodiles and bandits lurk, with the King's guards hot on their heels. Readers will find themselves on the edge of their seats, unable to put the book down as they are enticed through each chapter from one cliffhanger to the next. Readers will come to love the intrepid gang of young heroes, the dangerous setting and the exciting twists and turns in the plot.

It is a story or friendship, bravery, justice and adventure with a message of hope that, when everyone pulls together, change can happen.

About the author

The Girl Who Stole an Elephant is Nizrana Farook's debut children's book. As a child, she loved reading children's classics and writing her own stories. She always dreamed of being an author but only began her writing career much later in life when she decided to pursue her passion for writing seriously. Her other books include *The Boy Who Met a Whale* and *The Girl Who Lost a Leopard*.

She is originally from Colombo, the largest city on the island of Sri Lanka. Her experiences in the rainforests and on the beaches of Sri Lanka and love for the natural beauty of her homeland are an integral part of her stories.

She holds a master's degree in writing for children and lives in Hertfordshire with her husband and two daughters. She also runs workshops in schools on how to write adventure stories and visits schools for interactive talks with children about her stories and characters.

GUIDED READING ▶

Setting the scene

Introduce the book by encouraging the children to explore all the information on the book's cover (title, illustrations, reviews and blurb). Invite children to predict what they think the story will be about, as well as its genre. (It may not be initially clear from the cover that the book is classified as historical fiction.) Ask: *Who is the story's main protagonist? Why?* (Chaya; focus of the blurb) *What can you tell about the book's setting?* (village, jungle, possibly an island from the illustrations; suggests India or a similar part of the world)

Read the first chapter as a class, modelling expression for the dialogue and then inviting children to 'jump in' and continue reading. Invite volunteers to summarise the events of the first chapter. Discuss question 18 on the bookmark as a class, noting details that suggest the story is historical fiction (guards with spears, royal palaces and feasts, elephants). Keep a running list on the wall. Using question 14 on the bookmark, focus on the descriptive detail and rich language, asking volunteers to read out sentences or passages they found particularly vivid, and noting the powerful adjectives and verbs in the narrative. Explain that Serendib is a historical name for Sri Lanka, an island at the bottom of India, which confirms earlier predictions about the setting. As a class, discuss question 12 on the bookmark and identify the two reasons for italics in Chapter 1 (emphasis in dialogue and a foreign word – *'jambu'*, an exotic fruit). Survey the class to find out whether they found this a gripping beginning to a novel and why (for example, the first sentence takes the reader straight into the action).

Building up the plot and characters

Ask the children to read Chapter 2 in groups of three, with a narrator and the two characters, Chaya and Neel. Encourage fluency and expression and demonstrate how to 'read' an ellipsis (…) – either as a pause or an unfinished thought. At the

end, bring the class together and ask: *What do you think of Chaya's reasons for stealing the Queen's jewels?* Talk about plot elements that they have discovered and what they now know about Chaya and Neel. Discuss question 2 on the bookmark and then ask: *Why is Neel so worried about Chaya stealing the Queen's jewels?* (Chaya's father may get into trouble.) Invite volunteers to finish Neel's sentence, 'He will have your father—.' Ask: *How do you think Chaya feels at the end of the chapter?* (concerned that others may suffer because of her theft) *Why didn't she think of this before?* (She's headstrong; only thinking of the good she could do.) Discuss as a class question 17 on the bookmark, asking the children to keep this question in mind as the story progresses.

Read to the end of Chapter 4. Ask: *What is the challenge or problem to be solved in the plot?* (People are suffering as a result of Chaya's theft of the jewels. Someone has bought the box with the hidden jewels, so Chaya must get them back to return them and stop the suffering.) Ask: *What does it mean that the merchant was speaking slowly, 'Chaya's language sounding strange on his tongue'?* (He's speaking it as a foreign language, probably with an accent.) Ask the children to predict what Chaya is planning at the end of Chapter 4. Read Chapter 5 together and discuss question 15 on the bookmark as Chaya sneaks around the house searching for the box (active verbs, italics, short paragraphs, climax ending). Point out two more uses of italics for thoughts and Nour's note. Also note the building of textual emphasis in 'No. *No*. NO!' followed by short sentences and Chaya's discovery at the end of the chapter. Ask: *What do you think Chaya is feeling as she reads the note?*

Read Chapter 6 to the class, modelling expression and fluency, particularly in Chaya, Neel and Nour's conversation, underlining the absurdity of Chaya calling Nour a thief. Referring to questions 8 and 15 on the bookmark, focus on the chapter's final paragraph and its impact. Briefly revise the term 'cliffhanger' and encourage the children to imagine each character's thoughts and feelings as 'fear slashed deep into Chaya's heart'.

Trouble

Ask the children to read to the end of Chapter 10 in groups, thinking particularly about Chaya's dilemma and why everyone, including Chaya's father, assumes Neel must be guilty. Ask: *Why did Neel confess, knowing he would be sentenced to death?* (to protect his friend, Chaya) Read to the end of Chapter 16, focusing on questions 7 and 8 on the bookmark, encouraging the children to appreciate the cliffhanger technique at the end of each short chapter, noticing how it entices the reader into reading on while maintaining tension. Discuss together question 4 on the bookmark (lonely, outsider, envies their friendship) and how this relates to situations the children themselves may have been in, for example a new person in their class or community, or someone from a different country or culture wanting to find new friends. Ask: *Why is Chaya so contemptuous of Nour and her offer to help?* (She's from a different background/ class/culture; sees her as a nuisance/liability.) *How is this different to how Mahanama sees her?* (He's interested by the different culture, with all it has to offer.) Consider question 3 on the bookmark and talk about Chaya's plan to free Neel. Ask: *Had she thought it through carefully?* (no – a lot still unknown) *What does this tell you about Chaya?* (fearless, passionate, loyal, foolhardy, resourceful, brave, determined) *Why does Nour say to Chaya 'you're on your own'?* (Chaya wants everything her way; doesn't understand teamwork or sharing.) *Does she have a point?* Invite volunteers to explain how in fact they only managed to escape using teamwork – including Ananda!

Read Chapter 17 together. Ask: *How is each character feeling by the end of the chapter?* (determined, frightened, guilty, unsure) *What is their challenge?* (to undo everything and get the King to forgive or forget) Invite the children to predict how

they might resolve their situation. Ask: *Have you ever been in a situation where you have needed to right something you've done wrong?* Ask the children to read to the end of Chapter 19, focusing on question 16 on the bookmark noting how the author uses dialogue to provide background information about the characters, elephants and the setting, as well as transmit themes and messages through what the children learn about each other and themselves. Return to question 1 on the bookmark; ask: *Do the reasons Chaya gives Nour for stealing justify her actions?* Discuss question 5 on the bookmark and ask: *Why wouldn't the King understand Chaya 'helping' his people?*

The chase

Ask children to read Chapters 20 to 23 in groups, working on expression and fluency to add to the drama of the chase and listing both the animals they encounter and any dramatic events. Discuss together how the author builds tension and drama through the short chapters, the climaxes, the dialogue and the various disasters that beset the trio. Ask: *How did they escape the leopard?* (no sudden movements) *How would you feel if your legs were covered in leeches? What does Nour reveal about why she came?* (She wanted friends.) *Do you think this changes how Chaya regards Nour? How?* (yes – a little; more sympathetic) Encourage the children to empathise with each character in turn: Nour, lonely and in unfamiliar terrain tentatively making friends; Chaya realising it's not all about her, actions have consequences, and everyone makes mistakes; Neel feeling responsible for the girls. Consider the Chapter 23 climax. Ask: *Where and why has Neel gone?*

Read to the end of Chapter 27. Ask: *Do you think Chaya would have pushed Nour down the waterfall if she'd known that Nour couldn't swim?* Encourage the children to back up their ideas with evidence relating to what they know about Chaya. Then ask: *What might have happened if she hadn't pushed Nour?* (They'd have been caught by the King's soldiers, with dire consequences for everyone, including their families.) *If she had to, how do you think Chaya would answer Nour's question about going back and undoing everything?*

Bandits

Before reading on, invite volunteers to explain what a bandit is (an armed thief) and whether bandits are usually good or bad. Now read together to the end of Chapter 32, using the jumping-in technique with children. Ask: *What important information do the children learn?* (No one's yet dead; Chaya's father has been arrested; the King's half-brother, the banished Prince Sena, is preparing to overthrow the King, backed by bandits; the villagers blame the children for their troubles.) Review question 6 on the bookmark, asking: *Do the bandits now seem good or bad? Why?* Encourage the children to give reasons for how they answer (they don't harm the children, or steal Ananda's tusks). Ask the children to read Chapter 33 independently and predict what Mangala meant when he said Sena might not be what they were expecting. After reading Chapter 34 to the class, talk about question 10 on the bookmark. Remind the children how nobody believed a girl could have stolen the jewels and ask: *Why do you think the Princess was hiding her true identity?* Review other occasions when people assumed girls could not do things (Gamage also assumed Neel was the mastermind behind everything, as did Chaya's aunty and father).

Read to the end of Chapter 37. Ask: *Why do they go to Neel's area of the village?* (Rich city people won't join the uprising, Chaya's father has been arrested and poor people have suffered the most.) *How do you think the villagers will react to Chaya, Nour and Neel? How would you react in their situation?*

Resolution

Read Chapters 38 to 42 with the children. Ask: *What did the villagers want to do with Chaya and Neel?* (take them to the King) *How did the fire make things worse?* (People panicked, thinking Chaya and Neel were with the bandits and responsible for it.)

Read on to the end of the story with the class, modelling fluency and expression and then inviting children to jump in and read. Ask: *Why did the villagers change their minds about Chaya and her friends in front of the King?* (Nour persuades them that Chaya rang the bell to save the village and then they start to remember how she's helped so many of them.) *Even though Chaya was a thief, how did the proverb 'One good turn deserves another' apply to Chaya in the end?* (People remembered how she'd helped them when their King should have looked after them.) In the final chapter, Chaya claims she has changed; Neel says she hasn't. As a class, discuss question 20 on the bookmark and come to a class conclusion on who is right, backed by reasons.

Talk about the structure of the book as a whole, focusing on questions 9, 11 and 13 on the bookmark to guide your discussion. Encourage the children to skim back over the book to find passages or chapters to share with the class that support their ideas. Talk about the differences between first- and third-person narrative. Ask: *How would this book have been different if one of the characters had narrated the story?* Survey the class to find out which narrative person they generally prefer.

Ask the children to talk about question 19 on the bookmark in small groups before bringing the class together to share ideas for themes they identified (friendship, identity, loyalty, teamwork, power, morality and righting wrongs, a hero's journey). Discuss what each character learned on their adventure, about themselves and about others, and then ask the children which character they identified with the most and why. Finally, discuss with the class whether they think this book would have been as powerful in getting its messages across if it had been in a modern setting or a local setting. End by asking the children for any other proverbs that could apply to the story beyond 'One good turn deserves another' (such as 'Never judge a book by its cover' or 'All's well that ends well').

The Girl Who Stole an Elephant

by Nizrana Farook

Focus on...
Meaning

1. Why does Chaya steal things? Does her motive make it right?

2. Why is Neel working and not at school if he is only 13?

3. How does Chaya create a diversion outside the prison? Why does she do this?

4. Why does Nour decide to help Chaya and Neel?

5. Why are the people unhappy with the King and Queen? Are the people justified?

6. Are the bandits good or bad people?

Focus on...
Organisation

7. What is the effect of having so many short chapters in the book?

8. How does the author make you want to read on at the end of each chapter?

9. Explain how the novel follows standard story structure.

10. What is the big twist in the story? Did you anticipate it?

11. How does the end of the book link back to its beginning?

The Girl Who Stole an Elephant

by Nizrana Farook

Focus on...
Language and features

12. Explain the different reasons why some words in the text are in italics.

13. How would the story be different if it was in first-person narrative?

14. How does the author bring scenes and situations to life vividly? What sort of words help her?

15. What techniques does the author use to create tension, especially in the action and chase scenes?

16. Explain how the author uses dialogue to tell much of the story and express its messages.

Focus on...
Purpose, viewpoints and effects

17. Why does everybody assume a girl could not have stolen the Queen's jewels? What does this tell you about life in Serendib at that time?

18. What details tell you that this novel is historical fiction?

19. What themes run through the book? Which do you think is the most important?

20. Do you think Chaya is changed at the end of the story? Why?

SHARED READING ▶

Extract 1

- Read Extract 1. Ask the children to summarise what happens (Chaya flees, leaving scenes of chaos).

- Circle 'shimmied', 'shards' and 'pandemonium'. Explain each word in everyday language using the Focus word table from the supporting online resource (see page 5). Provide definitions for other words children may find tricky (for example, 'mahout', 'pouch', 'clusters', 'dais', 'promenade', 'running amok'), also using everyday language.

- Underline 'Chaya shimmied up the tree, hands scratching against the rough bark'. Ask: *What visual detail does the author's choice of 'shimmied' provide over 'climbed' in this sentence?* (smoothness and speed of the climb) Note the spelling rule (changing 'y' to 'i' before adding the suffix) as 'shimmied' derives from 'shimmy'. Discuss other contexts when 'shimmy' or 'shimmied' may be used.

- Invite volunteers to describe the jewels in Chaya's lap. Explain that 'shards' normally refer to broken pieces of glass or pottery. Ask: *What is broken here?* (coloured light reflecting on the jewels through the branches) Now invite synonyms for 'shard' ('fragments', 'slivers', 'pieces', 'splinters') and survey whether any are as effective.

- Review the use of powerful verbs in the extract. In groups, ask the children to re-read the extract, focusing on fluency and expression, underlining interesting verbs, noting how they add visual detail – for example, movement ('ran', 'dashed', 'flying', 'sprinted', 'running amok') or image-building ('sparkled', 'crunched', 'peering', 'roaring', 'trumpeted').

Extract 2

- Read Extract 2 to the children, modelling fluency and expression. Together, analyse different aspects of the reading and discuss how you approached them in your modelling: the dialogue, the single-line or short paragraphs, the inverted commas inside the dialogue, the dash at the end of a sentence, the italics.

- Ask the children to annotate their copies using underlining, notes and colours to remind them how to approach the reading. Use questions to stimulate discussion and assess comprehension as you work through the extract: *What's the reason for the inverted commas around 'sort of disappear'?* (repetition of Chaya's words) *What tone does it imply Nour uses in her question?* (almost sarcastic, emphasising the inherent contradiction in Chaya's words) *How would you describe their conversation?* (irritated with each other – Nour has had enough of Chaya's dismissive attitude) *Why doesn't Nour finish her final sentence?* (she's interrupted by Mahanama) *What might she have been going to say?* (that she would not leave) *What age is Mahanama?* (old) *How do you know?* (shuffles, stooped, calls her 'dear') *How would you speak his words in character?* (soft voiced, gentle) *What sort of person is he?* (monk in a temple) *How would Chaya speak differently to him than to Nour?* (respectful to her teacher/master) *Why did Chaya shudder at the word 'friend'?* (doesn't yet consider Nour a friend – more a necessary nuisance)

- Now ask the children to read the extract in groups of four, using their notes and enhanced understanding to bring the passage to life using expression, gestures and body language to support the characters' words and the context.

Extract 3

- Before reading, invite volunteers to summarise the plot so far. Now ask the children to read the extract silently before regrouping to contextualise the extract in terms of standard story structure: introduction, problem/challenge, build up, climax, conclusion/resolution. Ask: *What is happening in this extract?* (chase scene in jungle) Invite learners to volunteer words to describe the extract's atmosphere (tense, fast-paced, chaotic). Now read Extract 3 together, asking readers to jump in at appropriate moments.

- Discuss the author's techniques for building tension and enhancing the reader's experience. Ask: *What senses does the author draw on?* (touch, smell, taste, hearing, vision) Invite the children to underline examples in the extract to share with the class (for example, Chaya crushing mint leaves and inhaling the aroma; 'twitch of the owl and rustling of leaves'; 'With a great sound of hooves, horsemen erupted into view'). Ask: *What verbs heighten the tension through vivid imagery?* ('whispered', 'erupted', 'vaulted', 'flash', 'vibrated', 'pounding', 'burst', 'screamed') Ask the children to circle adverbs used in the text and discuss their impact. (Nour drinking 'greedily' depicts their exertion and heightened awareness of how close their chasers are; Neel listening 'intently' underlines how tense they are, and so on.)

- Point out that this extract is the end of Chapter 23. Ask: *What is the effect of the last two single-sentence paragraphs?* (a cliffhanger; the short paragraphs heighten the sense of panic and danger)

- At the end, encourage the children to share their ideas and predictions for what will happen next, both immediately and in the rest of the story, using words such as: *I believe that... I predict...*, supported by evidence from the text and their knowledge of story structure.

Extract 4

- Hand out enlarged copies of Extract 4 and invite the children to skim the text for features to help identify the text type (non-fiction, factual) and scan for specific words that support this (names, dates). Clarify the difference between non-fiction and fiction and discuss similarities between non-fiction and historical fiction (setting may be real, but characters and story may not be).

- Organise children for paired reading. Children can read together or take turns to read a sentence each. As they read, walk around and encourage them to support each other if they get stuck or make an error.

- Ask children to identify the audience (school children), purpose (background information about a country), language (formal, factual) and layout (headings, paragraphs, bullet points). Discuss how purpose is linked to layout, and audience is linked to language.

- Explain the meaning of topic-specific words: 'equator', 'monsoon', 'fauna', 'flora' and 'evergreen'. Explore focus words from the text such as 'dense', 'sophisticated', 'irrigate', 'livelihood', 'scenic'. Use the Focus word table from the supporting online resource (see page 5) to provide everyday explanations and dictionary definitions, then ask children to use the words in different contexts in sentences.

- Afterwards, children practise note-taking skills. Using coloured markers, they highlight the headings and key words, focusing on important nouns, verbs and adjectives. They then create a mind map of the information. Children can use their mind maps to recall the information to each other as a separate oral activity or write an information paragraph in their own words to show their understanding of the text.

- Bring the class back together for a quiz to check which facts they remember from this text.

Extract 1

"Stop!" The mahout waved his arms at the guards. "The elephants are getting disturbed."

The guards slowed down and Chaya took her chance. She ran to the boundary and dashed out through the gates. She was free.

Skirting the city, she headed towards the patches of wilderness on the east side of the palace, the wind flying through her hair as she sprinted away.

When she got there she stopped and leaned against a tree, catching her breath. She peered through the wilderness and smiled.

She'd lost them.

Chaya shimmied up the tree, hands scratching against the rough bark. She settled herself in one of the high branches and picked out the coconut blossoms stuck in her hair. Lifting her linen pouch over her neck, she dropped the jewels into her lap. They sparkled in shards of bright blue, green and pink against the grey of her skirt.

It had been a huge risk. Her boldest robbery to date. And yet she'd pulled it off.

She picked a jambu fruit from a branch nearby and crunched into its juicy pink flesh, peering through the leaves at the royal compound in the distance.

It was pandemonium down there. The crowds were scattered and panicked, clusters of people moving in different directions. The King, standing out in his gold-encrusted waistcoat, had come down from the dais and was roaring at his staff. The Queen and her procession of ladies were being guided out of the promenade up to the palace. The mahouts on the green were trying desperately to calm their confused charges and stop them running amok. In the middle of it all, Ananda lifted up his majestic head and trumpeted loudly into the blue, blue sky.

Extract 2

Chaya looked around the compound as she tugged off her shoes. No one was within earshot. The monk in the compound stamped the broom on the ground and went round to the back. "So I go in with you. If anyone asks, you know why we're here. Me, I'm going to sort of disappear."

…

"What does 'sort of disappear' even mean?" said Nour. "Either you disappear or you don't."

"Fine, I'm going to disappear."

"Where to?"

"That," said Chaya, making for an arched passage, "is none of your business."

"In *that* case," Nour started back towards the entrance, "you're on your own."

"Hey!" Chaya ran up behind Nour, her voice echoing through the passage. "What's wrong with you? You said you wanted to help."

"I do. But you want to do everything your own way."

Chaya was confused. "So?"

"So you can't expect people to help if you don't tell them things."

"Why not? Once I disappear, your part's over." Chaya made a slashing action with her hand to emphasise the *over*. "I only need you as a reason to *be* in the temple. Once I'm gone, you can leave."

"Leave?"

"Yeah. Go home. Go for a walk. Eat those sugary sweets on your sideboard. Whatever."

Nour scowled. "I'm not going to—"

"Chaya?" Soft footsteps padded down the curving passage and her teacher Mahanama shuffled into view. "Is that you, dear?"

Chaya glared at Nour. This would never have happened if Nour had just done as she was told and not argued. "Yes, Master."

"What are you doing here so early? It's not Friday, is it?" He peered at Nour, readjusting his robe over one stooping shoulder. "Who is your friend?"

Chaya shuddered at *friend*. "This is Nour, Master. Her father is the merchant, Cassim. I've brought her to see our temple."

 # Extract 3

Chaya picked at some wild mint leaves while they waited, crushing them in her fingers and inhaling their aroma. A squashed-looking owl the colour of dried leaves roosted in a branch overhead.

Neel handed Nour the pitcher of water he was carrying and she drank greedily.

"Thank you," she whispered.

"Wait a minute." Neel held up a hand and listened intently. "Oh no. Not again."

Chaya pricked up her ears. All she heard was the twitch of the owl and rustling of leaves.

"They're here," said Neel. "Come on. Nour, get up."

Chaya looked back. They could see only about thirty feet behind them. "I don't hear anything," she said.

"Trust me, they're here. They've got to be close."

With a great sound of hooves, horsemen erupted into view in the distance. Neel was off like a hare, pulling Nour by her wrist. Chaya sprinted after them. The jungle was sparse here, the horses easily catching up with them.

Chaya vaulted over a fallen tree. She saw Nour's dress flash ahead and kept up with her. The thuds of horse hooves were getting closer. She knew Nour was already tired. It was only minutes before they'd be captured, surely.

The horsemen were practically at her back. The hoof beats vibrated through Chaya, pounding into her head. She burst ahead, almost passing Nour but slowed down for her.

She couldn't see Neel anywhere.

"Where's Neel?" Chaya screamed. Nour looked around in terror, but kept on ahead. The horsemen seemed to have divided, some of them going off in another direction.

Chaya looked around wildly. A group of horsemen were chasing something on the far left. They disappeared from sight as she pounded after Nour, a small army of guards at their back.

Chaya and Nour were alone in the jungle, being chased by the King's guards.

And Neel was gone.

Extract 4

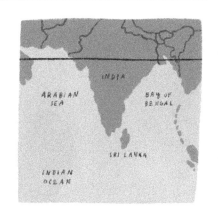

Sri Lanka

Location

Sri Lanka is an island in the Indian Ocean, south of India.
In ancient times it was a popular stop-over for traders
from other countries.

Sri Lanka is near to the equator, with a warm, wet climate and heavy rainfall in
the south-west. The southern area has many rivers and mountains and is covered
with thick, dense, tropical forests. Monsoons cause heavy rain, wind and sometimes
flooding on the island. The northern areas are much drier. A sophisticated watering
system helps to irrigate crops.

Historical names

Sri Lanka was called Taprobane by the ancient Greeks, Serendib in Arabia and
later European mapmakers called it Ceylon. It officially became Sri Lanka in 1972.

Fauna and flora

The rainforest is home to tropical plants and trees such as the blue water lily
and Ceylon ironwood. Animals include the Sri Lankan elephant and leopard,
wild hare, jungle shrew, flying squirrel, Ceylon junglefowl (the national bird)
and peacocks.

Elephants are used for logging and to attract tourists to national parks. They
used to roam wild but are now protected in national parks.

Fast facts:
- The official languages are Sinhala and Tamil.
- The majority of people farm for their livelihood.
- Popular crops include rice, tea and coconuts.
- The evergreen cinnamon tree, thought to be used by the ancient
  Egyptians, is native to Sri Lanka.

Things to do:
- Take the train from Kandy to Ella through
  the scenic mountains, forests and plantations.
- Visit the national parks to see the country's
  protected wildlife.

GRAMMAR, PUNCTUATION & SPELLING ▶

1. Tell me more

Objective
To use expanded noun phrases.

What you need
Copies of *The Girl Who Stole an Elephant*, photocopiable page 22 'Tell me more'.

What to do

- Revise phrases: groups of words without a verb working together as adjectives, adverbs or nouns. Explain that noun phrases tell us more in a neat, concise way about the head/main noun.

- Write 'sweet' (noun) on the board and invite adjectives to describe one, encouraging interesting words. Draw a mind map surrounding 'sweet', noting whether words describe its look, taste, smell or texture. Practise describing the sweet using adjectives separated by a comma; *It was a (adjective, adjective) sweet*. Now add more description after 'sweet': *It was a… sweet with…* such as *with a chewy, chocolate coating*.

- Write a basic word pattern on the board: *A/The adjective, adjective noun with (the/a) adjective, noun* and ask small groups to invent noun phrases for 'house', 'garden' and 'bed'. Invite groups to share their most descriptive ones. Note determiners form part of the phrase.

- Work though the Chapter 5 sentence describing the delicious-smelling sweet on the board (*There was some kind of fried sweet, coated with powdered sugar, still warm and smelling of syrup*), demonstrating how the noun phrase expands with elements before and after the head noun.

- Ask children to complete photocopiable page 22 'Tell me more'.

Differentiation
Support: Children need to only complete the first part of the photocopiable page.

Extension: Children skim Chapter 5 for expanded noun phrases to share with the class.

2. Missing or interrupted?

Objective
To understand ellipsis.

What you need
Copies of *The Girl Who Stole an Elephant*.

What to do

- Write 'ellipsis'/'ellipses' and its punctuation mark (…) on the board, linking the irregular plural to its ancient Greek origins. Invite words with similar plurals ('oasis', 'basis', 'crisis', 'thesis').

- Remind children that ellipses usually represent missing words or mark a pause. Then ask them to read Chapter 4 from '"But I insist," said Neel' to the end. Point out the carpenter's unfinished statement, "And you, boy, another word from you…" Ask: *What was the carpenter implying? How would you complete what he was saying?* (you'll be in terrible trouble) Then ask: *What's the effect of the ellipsis in Nour's words "And it's also…"?* (shows she pauses while looking at Chaya before continuing)

- Now ask: *Why is there a dash at the end of Neel's words "That's not accept—"?* (interrupted before he can finish) Explain that the author often uses a long dash rather than '…' to indicate omitted words or a pause for effect.

- Ask groups to study Chapter 6, focusing on the ellipses before reading the chapter aloud. To enhance their reading, ask: *What's the purpose of each ellipsis?* (interrupted speech/unspoken words) Encourage them to ask what might have been said and why the author chose the dash or ellipsis, and to look for a pattern.

Differentiation
Support: Work with groups to practise the dialogue, especially interrupting.

Extension: Groups skim other chapters to explore patterns in ellipsis use (Chapters 2, 7, 11, 44).

3. Spell it right

Objective

To distinguish between homophones.

What you need

Copies of *The Girl Who Stole an Elephant*, slips of paper, photocopiable page 23 'Spell it right'.

What to do

- First, revise homophones. List some on the board, for example: 'right', 'heard', 'scent', 'threw'. Invite volunteers to suggest different ways to spell each word ('write', 'herd', 'sent', 'through'). Explain that words sounding the same but spelled differently with different meanings are homophones.

- Group the children and ask them to read the three paragraphs in Chapter 9 just after the chapter break ('Chaya clutched the paper bag…' to '"…I just need to see him one last time."'). Challenge them to find as many homophones as possible (at least 12). Survey how many each group find and bring the class back together to review their words and discuss alternative meanings.

- Now, hold a homophone challenge. Hand out slips of paper and give groups five minutes to think of pairs of homophones, writing each word pair on a separate slip of paper. Collect their papers and choose 10 random words from the pile. Say each homophone and ask children to write down all the possible spellings. Challenge groups to use the homophones in sentences to demonstrate that they can differentiate by using the words in context and then ask them to identify each homophone's word class.

- Ask the children to complete photocopiable page 23. Invite volunteers to read out their sentence pairs.

Differentiation

Support: Provide a list of homophones matching the text to help children find the originals.

Extension: Pairs can choose another chapter or passage, with each scanning for homophones before comparing findings.

4. Working with words

Objective

To discuss and explore the meaning of words in context.

What you need

Focus word table from the shared reading of Extract 1, Extract 1, dictionaries and thesauruses.

What to do

- Mix up and display copies of the focus words ('shimmied', 'shards', 'pandemonium') and their everyday definitions. Ask children to match words and definitions.

- Organise children in groups. Explain that they will take turns to respond to these prompts: *Think of three unusual things that you could have 'shimmied' up. Think of three things that might break or shatter into 'shards'. Describe three moments when you have experienced 'pandemonium'.* Listen to groups working. Choose interesting responses and ask children to share them with the class, reflecting on how the activity helps build understanding of the target words and the different contexts in which they might be used.

- Now, ask children to use the target words in their own sentences, choosing their favourite to read aloud. Discuss their sentences and the impact of the target words.

- Broaden the children's understanding of the target words further by drawing a target on the board with 'pandemonium' as the bull's eye in the centre. Invite volunteers to suggest words with similar meanings (allow them to use dictionaries and thesauruses). Start with a couple of your own (examples could include 'chaos', 'mayhem', 'uproar', 'hubbub', 'confusion', 'disorder', 'commotion'). Ask the children to judge how close or far from the bull's eye to write each word based on how close they judge the similar word's meaning to be.

- Write the target words on the working wall, reminding the children to aim to use them in their written work.

Differentiation

Support: Ask children to devise sentences in pairs.

Extension: Groups can do the synonym/target activity on paper with the other target words.

5. Join the clauses

Objective
To use colons, semicolons and dashes to separate independent clauses.

What you need
Copies of *The Girl Who Stole an Elephant*, photocopiable page 24 'Join the clauses'.

What to do

- Revise independent and dependent clauses (independent clauses can stand alone). Ask: *How do you separate independent clauses in compound (multi-clause) sentences?* Discuss answers such as using a coordinating conjunction (use the acronym 'FANBOYS': 'for', 'and', 'nor', 'because', 'or', 'yet', 'so') or an adverb preceded by a comma or a semicolon; or just punctuation (colon, semicolon or dash).

- Explain when to use a colon or a semicolon. Colons introduce another related idea, illustrating the first clause. Semicolons indicate a close relationship, with the second clause continuing the idea. However, as with parenthesis, dashes can be used, in this case, in place of colons or semicolons. Modern writers sometimes use dashes to join independent clauses to show a change in tone or add additional information. However, it is considered more informal and writers in the past are unlikely to have used dashes in this way; even now they shouldn't be over-used.

- Ask pairs to read Chapter 5 to identify three compound sentences: two joined by dashes and one by a semicolon (note the colon introduces a noun for emphasis – not a clause). Ask: *Why do you think the author used dashes in the first two?* (additional information and also a tone-change in the second) *How is the sentence with the semicolon different?* (equally weighted, closely related – the second clause continuing the thought)

- Hand out photocopiable page 24 'Join the clauses' for children to complete. Encourage them to explain their reasoning.

Differentiation
Support: Children can work in pairs.

Extension: Ask children to skim other chapters for examples of independent clauses joined just by punctuation and add these to the working wall.

6. Speaking is different

Objective
To explore informal speech.

What you need
Copies of *The Girl Who Stole an Elephant*.

What to do

- Revise the main differences between dialogue and narrative (tenses, formality/register, flexible grammar, contractions, use of slang and colloquial expressions, inversion, question tags and so on).

- Read Chapter 11 with the class, modelling fluency and expression, especially in the dialogue, asking children to jump in. While reading, ask them to focus on dialogue to note how it differs from narrative. Ask: *What informal or slang words did you notice?* ('OK'; 'Hey!'; 'Yeah'; 'Ah'; contractions such as 'I'm'; 'sweet-as-jaggery' – jaggery is unrefined brown sugar made from palm sap)

- Organise the children into groups and divide up the chapter, giving a section to each group. Ask them to scan their section, this time looking for informal phrases or constructions unlikely to be used in more formal narrative text. Start with an example such as the use of 'So' at the beginning of speech: 'So I go in with you.'; 'So you can't expect people…'.

- Bring the class together to discuss their findings on the board, classifying them as far as possible under headings, for example, use of italics/text effects ('In *that* case'; 'What *act*?'), single word sentences ('Whatever.'), interruptions ('I'm not going to—'), question tags ('is it?'), command verbs ('Come on'), informal phrases ('you know'), ellipses for pauses, question marks turning statements into questions ('Miss Chaya?'). Finally, ask: *Does Mahanama speak like the girls? Why?* (No – he's more formal; in keeping with his age and being a monk; giving advice.) Encourage examples: "Is that you dear?", "Remember to also be a kind person."

Differentiation
Support: Give children just one or two features to focus on.

Extension: Children can role play by adding to the dialogue between Chaya and Nour.

Tell me more

- Circle the head noun and underline the expanded noun phrase in each sentence below.

1. The large, single-storeyed house with a paved verandah was an easy target.

2. It had a tiny, well-tended garden, with sprays of pink bougainvillea.

3. Next came a comfortable, airy bedroom with floaty, patterned curtains.

4. It had a small, four-poster bed, with a leather trunk at its foot.

5. The room had an intense, exotic smell like summer jasmine in the evening.

- Create expanded noun phrases following this pattern: *adjective, adjective, (adjective) noun with (a/the) adjective noun*

  1. _____, _____ doorway with

     _____ _____

  2. _____, _____ box with _____

     _____

  3. _____, _____, _____

     market with _____ _____

- Write a sentence to include one of the expanded noun phrases above.

  _____

  _____

  _____

Spell it right

- Write a sentence using each word in the correct context. Use a dictionary to check your work.

1. through _____

2. threw _____

3. see _____

4. sea _____

5. we'll _____

6. wheel _____

7. wail _____

8. whale _____

9. to _____

10. too _____

11. two _____

12. been _____

13. bean _____

14. one _____

15. won _____

Join the clauses

- Choose the best punctuation from the box to join the independent clauses. Explain your choice underneath.

;	:	—

1. People were in a good mood___ they wouldn't expect a thief tonight!

_____

2. Chaya had one choice___ push Nour over the waterfall.

_____

3. They were trapped___ it was the end.

_____

4. The jungle had many creatures___ it had leopards, monkeys, leeches and more.

_____

5. The steps were blocked___ she couldn't get there.

_____

6. Write your own compound sentences using the punctuation shown to link the independent clauses.

(—) _____

_____

(;) _____

_____

(:) _____

_____

PLOT, CHARACTER & SETTING ▶

1. Dialogue to tell the story

Objective
To evaluate how authors use dialogue.

What you need
Copies of *The Girl Who Stole an Elephant*.

What to do

• Ask: *Why do authors include dialogue in stories?* (It brings the story to life, advances the action, builds characters.) *How do readers know how words are spoken?* (infer from context, actual words, punctuation, verbs – 'said' or synonyms/ adverbs – or action in narrative)

• Organise groups to read Chapter 6, focusing on how the author indicates the way words are spoken, noting examples to share with the class. Start with an example from the first paragraph: '"Can you *believe it*? How dare she!" Chaya paced the workshop.' (italics; exclamation mark; the character's action is described – 'paced' – but there is no reporting clause). Then discuss what it reveals about Chaya (volatile, impatient, impulsive).

• Often, the author doesn't use a reporting clause ('said Chaya') because the speaker is assumed from the context. Ask: *How does this bring the story to life?* (It is more like real conversations, which don't have a narrator popping up.) Encourage groups to role play the dialogue, using the narrative to inform their expression and body language before discussing what the dialogue reveals about the three main characters and the plot.

• End by asking: *Do you think people in this setting would have spoken like Chaya, Nour and Neel?* (probably not; the dialogue seems quite modern, but it helps readers relate to the characters)

Differentiation
Support: Limit the number of pages children study.

Extension: Children repeat the activity with another dialogue-rich chapter.

2. Serendib

Objective
To investigate the setting.

What you need
Copies of *The Girl Who Stole an Elephant*, Extract 4, large card, colours.

Cross-curricular link
Geography

What to do

• Read Chapter 1 from 'In spite of everything…' to 'little villages beyond' to contextualise the overall setting for the story. Now, ask the children to read Extract 4 to learn more about the island of Serendib (modern-day Sri Lanka). Ask: *How does this setting sound different from where you live?* Use their responses to list similarities and differences. Ask: *Where would you prefer to live? Why?*

• Ask groups to research the jungle setting. They should skim through the story from Chapters 17 to 27 to draw information from different places. Ask them to make notes on scenery, weather, trees, food, animals and water, also noting sounds, smells and tastes. Encourage them to think about what the characters eat and drink, where they sleep and how they solve problems (such as making a fire, cooking). Ask them to choose favourite passages to read out illustrating the characters' experiences in the jungle (for example, the leeches).

• Ask the children to make a mind map of their notes on large card to include facts, descriptive words and phrases and illustrations to bring this part of the story to life. Display their mind maps.

Differentiation
Support: Give groups limited settings to research: the King's palace, the temple or Nour's house.

Extension: Children prepare a presentation on the Serendib jungle, based on their mind maps.

PLOT, CHARACTER & SETTING

3. Then and now

Objective
To make comparisons within and across books.

What you need
Copies of *The Girl Who Stole an Elephant*.

Cross-curricular links
History, PSHE

What to do

- Discuss historical fiction. Survey class books or books the children have read in this genre and elicit general features to write on the board: authentic background details; invented scenes, characters and dialogue; social, religious and cultural attitudes and values relevant to the period; realistic historical settings, technology, buildings, clothes, travel.

- Organise the children into groups to explore the book's historical details. Ask: *What is the main setting? What details reveal it isn't set in modern times?* (For example, the King, guards, Neel leaving school before age 13.)

- Now encourage the children to compare the book's setting with their own lives and other books they have read set in the modern day. Ask: *What are the biggest differences to your life or the lives of characters in other modern novels?* (for example, technology) Encourage groups to discuss their ideas, using evidence and examples from the story, other books and their lives. Hold a plenary to share each group's ideas.

- End by focusing on one of the plot's primary contextual issues. Ask: *Why did no one think Chaya could have stolen the jewels?* (because she is a girl) *Who made this assumption?* (guards, General Siri, King, Father, Aunty, bandits, villagers) *What does this say about life in that society and time?* Be sensitive in the discussion not to make judgements but rather to note how things were different and how Chaya took advantage of the prevailing beliefs.

Differentiation
Support: Give learners specific areas to focus on, such as the buildings or the guards.

Extension: Children can explore why Leela kept her identity secret and why the King was more worried about Sena than her.

4. Grabbing attention and satisfying endings

Objective
To identify how structure and presentation contribute to meaning.

What you need
Copies of *The Girl Who Stole an Elephant*, independent reading books.

What to do

- Invite volunteers to read out the openings of their independent readers. Survey the class to establish what makes a good beginning to a book, collating their ideas on the board.

- Now read the first two pages of *The Girl Who Stole an Elephant*, modelling fluency and expression. Ask: *Is this beginning attention-grabbing? Why?* (yes; dramatic scene with spear pointing at neck) *What have you learned about the story?* (main character, Chaya, is a thief; a palace with guards; likely to be historical)

- Discuss the book as a whole. Ask: *Why did the author divide it into so many chapters?* (maintains pace in the novel – each chapter is like a mini film-scene) *How do many of the chapters end?* (on cliffhangers) *Why?* (to keep reader engaged) Ask groups to skim through the novel and choose their favourite cliffhanger endings to share with the class, explaining why they chose them.

- Now, turn to the final chapter and read out the first line. Ask: *How does this link the beginning and end of the story?* (It is the same sentence.) *Has anything changed?* (different atmosphere and context; guard is friendly; Chaya's not in trouble) *How does this chapter provide a satisfactory conclusion to the story?* (reveals things are better under Queen Leela, Chaya is forgiven, children's bravery is recognised, Nour now has friends)

Differentiation
Support: Give selected children a specific chapter with a cliffhanger ending to discuss.

Extension: Children compare the beginnings and endings of their independent readers in groups, noting similarities or differences to *The Girl Who Stole an Elephant*.

5. Character building

Objective

To draw inferences about characters.

What you need

Copies of *The Girl Who Stole an Elephant*, photocopiable page 29 'Character building'.

What to do

- After reading Chapter 10, ask: *What impression do you get of Chaya, Neel and Nour so far?* They aren't described physically in detail, but their actions and dialogue gradually reveal their characters. Acknowledge all answers but look for reasoned views.

- Demonstrate using questions to check understanding and learn more about the characters and their motivation. Ask: *What problem do the characters face?* (Neel is sentenced to death for stealing the Queen's jewels.) *What is Chaya planning?* (to rescue Neel) *Why?* (It's her fault he's imprisoned.) *Why doesn't Neel say what really happened?* (He is loyal to his friend; no one would believe him.) *Why is Nour following Chaya?* (She is trying to help.) *Why does Nour want to help?* (Accept all reasoned answers.) *Why is Chaya dismissive of Nour's offer of help?* (She thinks Nour is rich and spoiled/knows nothing about real life.)

- Organise the class into groups and assign a character to each group. Hand out photocopiable page 29 'Character building' and explain that groups must gather evidence about their character to build a profile as they read/re-read the novel, discussing their character at various points in the story and using questions to analyse their character's actions, motivation and how they change – focusing on 'what' and 'why' questions and then on how the author reveals character: through narrative, dialogue and inference.

- At the end, groups can get together to discuss their characters using their questions as a prompt.

Differentiation

Support: Guide children to specific chapters for their character.

Extension: Groups could profile two or three characters or analyse Ananda as a character.

6. Vivid description

Objective

To discuss and evaluate how authors use language, considering the impact on the reader.

What you need

Copies of *The Girl Who Stole an Elephant*, photocopiable page 30 'Vivid description'.

What to do

- Together, read Chapter 26 from 'She opened her eyes' to the end of the chapter.

- Now, invite volunteers to summarise the past few chapters and then ask: *What techniques does the author use to show this is one of Chaya's lowest moments?* Model how to use evidence to support answers. For example: the variation of paragraph lengths reflects the pattern of Chaya's thoughts – listing each aspect of her situation; rhetorical questions reflect her confusion after her near-death experience; the natural world reflects her desperate state – butterfly wings cast shadows, chilly wind; she has cuts and tattered clothes; descriptive words and verbs – 'swirling', 'arced', 'translucent', 'fluttered', 'chilly', 'swept', 'shivered', 'stung', 'tattered', 'wincing', 'looming'. Ask: *How does the chapter end?* (on a feeling of hope; Chaya is not alone)

- Organise the class into pairs and hand out photocopiable page 30 'Vivid description'. Explain that they will use close reading to analyse the author's use of descriptive techniques in the next chapter, Chapter 27, to vividly depict the setting, the mood, the characters' feelings and development, and the action. They can choose one or more pages to study, noting techniques and examples of vivid description.

- Bring the class together to share their findings. Focus on techniques they can use in their writing.

Differentiation

Support: Explain the meaning of any unfamiliar words in everyday language and encourage the children to think of synonyms for those words, evaluating the impact of the different options.

Extension: Pairs can review the whole chapter and then analyse the techniques used in another chapter.

PLOT, CHARACTER & SETTING

7. Thinking about themes

> **Objective**
> To identify and discuss themes.
>
> **What you need**
> Copies of *The Girl Who Stole an Elephant*.
>
> **Cross-curricular link**
> PSHE

What to do

- Revise the difference between a book's plot (the storyline) and theme/s (the main idea/messages). Themes in children's literature often deal with ways to cope with common dilemmas, fears and hopes that children experience. Questions help identify themes: *What challenges do the characters face? What do they learn?* Write a few common themes on the board such as friendship, overcoming adversity, loyalty, being an outsider and so on. Build up a list of common themes using class or individual readers and questions. Discuss how messages in the story can apply in our own lives for us to learn from as well.

- Organise the children into groups to answer the question: *What themes underlie* The Girl Who Stole an Elephant? (For example, friendship, loyalty, the nature of right and wrong, teamwork, accepting different cultures, courage and overcoming fears, the class system.) Bring the class together to share their ideas using examples from the story, encouraging groups to build on each other's ideas while also listening respectfully. Write each theme on large card, with examples from the story.

- Broaden the discussion on themes to what we can learn from the story despite the different context, for example, understanding that everyone has their own talents and people should not be judged superficially on what they do, who they are, where they come from or what they know.

- Ask: *Which is the most important theme?* Decide as a class and make a wall display with the most important theme in the centre.

> **Differentiation**
> **Support:** Give selected groups a single theme to focus on.
>
> **Extension:** Children can write about which character they identify with most and why.

8. A hero's journey?

> **Objective**
> To identify and discuss conventions in and across writing.
>
> **What you need**
> Copies of *The Girl Who Stole an Elephant*, photocopiable page 31 'A hero's journey?'

What to do

- Briefly revise classic story structure (introduction, problem, build-up, climax, resolution, conclusion) and discuss how this story fits this pattern. Now introduce the 'heroic journey' (Joseph Campbell, *The Hero with a Thousand Faces* – monomyth): the archetypal story pattern of events found in both ancient myths and many modern 'hero' stories and films. Together discuss heroes in books and films the children know and then ask: *What qualities do you think a hero has?* (often a seemingly ordinary person who feels something is wrong or who's lost something; courageous; needs help; faces challenges; loyal and so on)

- Provide groups with photocopiable page 31 'A hero's journey?' and read the twelve common elements together, discussing any unfamiliar words. Explain that they are going to decide if Chaya's journey fits the pattern. Emphasise that not all stages need to be exact, but it should follow the general pattern: call, test, transformation, return. For example, there may not be a 'special world', but the jungle isn't their usual world; Ananda may not be supernatural aid, but he certainly represents help out of the ordinary. Remind the children that transformation isn't necessarily total so they must decide how Chaya is the same (steals General Siri's letter opener) as well as changed.

- Groups discuss their ideas on whether Chaya can be considered a 'hero' while making notes on a separate piece of paper.

- Bring the class back together to share the groups' ideas and conclusions.

> **Differentiation**
> **Support:** Children focus on one or two of the key stages: call, test, transformation, return.
>
> **Extension:** Children discuss how their own lives so far follow the hero's journey.

Character building

- Build up a character profile from descriptive words or phrases and other evidence (dialogue, actions/reactions, thoughts).

Character: _____

Questions (for example, *What problems does this character face?*)	Words, phrases, evidence

How he/she has changed and why: _____

Vivid description

- Find examples of the techniques used in Chapter 27 and write them in the table.
- Add your own technique with an example you have found.

Technique	Examples
Descriptive words and verbs	
Figurative language	
Rhetorical questions	
Punctuation and text effects	
Sentence length	

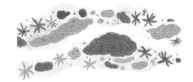

A hero's journey?

- Make notes on whether Chaya went on a hero's journey.

CALL

1. Ordinary world: hero's ordinary life

2. Call: something happens to shake things up to prompt the adventure

3. Assistance: hero finds help, often from unexpected places

TEST

4. Departure: hero enters other world of unknown rules and values

5. Trials: hero is tested – with unexpected challenges

6. Approach: hero and friends prepare for main challenge in other world

RETURN

12. Resolution: Life returns to a new normal

11. Return: completes quest, bearing gift or power to transform (world or self)

10. Atonement: climax – hero is tested a final time

TRANSFORMATION

9. Journey home: hero faces further danger on return

8. Result: hero and friends overcome challenges

7. Crisis: hero confronts death or greatest fears

TALK ABOUT IT ▶

1. Author Q & A

Objective
To use relevant questions to learn about the author.

What you need
Copies of *The Girl Who Stole an Elephant*, photocopiable page 35 'Author Q & A'.

What to do
- Organise the children into small discussion groups and provide each group with photocopiable page 35 'Author Q & A'. Begin by asking: *What do you know about the author?* Guide the children to use the book cover (inside and outside) to find clues. Invite responses.

- Read aloud the information about Nizrana Farook provided on page 8. Invite the children to recall the information they heard, collating their information into a mind map on the board about the author.

- In groups, children discuss the questions provided on the photocopiable sheet and fill in the answers together, as if they are the author being interviewed. Remind them to use the first person for this ('I grew up…'; 'I enjoy…') Encourage them to make up further questions they would like to ask the author about this book, considering the plot, setting, characters and so on. *(What is the story about? Where does it take place? What inspired you to write this story? Who is your favourite character? How did you come up with the title? What was your favourite part to write?)*

- Children can do further research to answer their questions.

Differentiation
Support: Provide further information from internet sites such as the publisher of the book's website (nosycrow.com).

Extension: Children role play an interview with the author using their notes.

2. Dialogue dilemmas

Objective
To explore and perform dialogue using appropriate registers.

What you need
Copies of *The Girl Who Stole an Elephant*.

What to do
- Begin by explaining the word 'dilemma' in everyday language (a predicament, a situation where you have to make a difficult choice – usually between equally unfavourable options). Ask: *Has anyone been in a dilemma where they didn't know what to do?* Invite responses.

- In small groups, invite the children to read the dialogue in Chapters 7 and 8 where the characters face dilemmas (how to save Neel, whether to tell Father). Identify the characters and the register – how they speak to each other. (Chapter 7 between Chaya and the guards and General Siri – desperate, cruel, unkind; and later between Chaya and Nour – impatient, irritated, familiar; Chapter 8 between Chaya and her father – unhappy, respectful, use of fatherly phrases like 'my child'.)

- Discuss and compare the difference in tone, degree of formality, choice of vocabulary, pronunciation and expression and consider how it varies depending on who is speaking to whom. Discuss why 'register' matters in dialogue. (In everyday speech we usually address people differently according to their role or position.)

- In pairs, children practise performing a dialogue from another chapter, focusing on who is speaking to whom and using appropriate tone and expression. Listen in on their dialogues and provide feedback and suggestions.

Differentiation
Support: Model reading the dialogue aloud.

Extension: Pairs invent and perform a dialogue with expression and body language.

3. Right or wrong?

Objective
To participate in debates about the issue of stealing.

What you need
Copies of *The Girl Who Stole an Elephant*, news articles about theft.

Cross-curricular link
PSHE

What to do
- Read Chapter 5 together as a choral reading, with groups for some sections and others as whole class reading. Ask: *How do you know Chaya is used to stealing?* Identify and discuss extracts such as 'Nobody ever noticed Chaya when she was dressed like this' and 'Chaya knew this was going to be easy'.

- Refer to other examples in the story where Chaya steals. Ask: *What are her reasons and motives for stealing?* (to help others) *What consequences does she face?* (prison) *Does her age matter?* (not in those days) Recall the story of Robin Hood (legendary hero in English folklore who stole from the rich to help the poor). Discuss links between Robin Hood and Chaya.

- Divide the class into two groups – one group to argue that it's right to steal if your motive is good and the other group to argue that it is always wrong.

- Allow time for groups to prepare their argument supported by examples from the story and, if possible, facts and quotes from other sources.

- Organise chairs in front of the class and give each group's chosen representatives an opportunity to speak. Afterwards, invite the audience to question the speakers, allowing time for responses from the speakers and the audience.

Differentiation
Extension: Children prepare a speech giving both sides of the argument, ending with a personal view.

4. Different but similar

Objective
To compare the different backgrounds and viewpoints of the characters.

What you need
Copies of *The Girl Who Stole an Elephant*, photocopiable page 36 'Different but similar'.

Cross-curricular link
PSHE

What to do
- Begin by asking: *Do you and your friends like the same films, eat the same food, enjoy the same things?* Discuss in groups things they enjoy doing together, things that are the same (like school) and things that are different (holidays, hobbies, families…)

- Skim extracts from Chapters 4, 11 and 16 to 22. Ask: *Where does Nour come from? What is different about her, and for her? In Chapter 21, why does Nour say 'I r-really hate this place'? What is she referring to? How do you think Nour feels about being 'the new kid' or 'the odd-one-out'?*

- In groups, ask the children to compare Chaya and Nour and identify their similarities (age, headstrong, adventurous) and differences in their characters and experiences. Ask the groups to use photocopiable page 36 'Different but similar' to make notes.

- Children now discuss how these differences affect their friendship. Ask: *Why was it difficult for them to be friends at first? What experiences do they share? Do they find common ground? What helps them be friends at the end? Do their differences really matter?* (At first, they clash but then they grow to understand each other.)

- Encourage children to report to the class using these sentence stems: *They're similar because… Things that make them different are… Nour feels different because… but she has similar…*

Differentiation
Extension: Children can compare other characters' similarities and differences, such as Neel and Chaya.

5. Helping hands

Objective
To participate in discussions about who helps whom in the story.

What you need
Copies of *The Girl Who Stole an Elephant*, photocopiable page 37 'Helping hands', Extract 2.

Cross-curricular link
PSHE

What to do

- Read Extract 2, inviting readers to 'jump in' when directed. Ask: *Why does Nour say to Chaya 'So you can't expect people to help if you don't tell them things'? What does Chaya not tell Nour? Why? Does Nour live by her own words?* (No, she doesn't always ask for help, for example, Chapter 24 where Chaya discovers Nour can't swim.) Ask: *Why doesn't Chaya want Nour's help?* (She's independent.) *Why does Nour want to help?* (She wants to be part of something.)

- Ask the children if friends always ask for help when in trouble and give reasons why sometimes they may not ask for help.

- Provide small groups with photocopiable page 37 'Helping hands' and guide them to discuss examples in the story of who helps whom and when, as well as how and why they help. Provide sentence stems on the board to aid discussion: *She helped…when…; He/She helped…because…; She didn't appreciate the help…; They needed help to…; She didn't ask for help because….* Come together and share ideas as a class.

- Finally, discuss the following colloquial expressions and how they relate to the story: 'lend a helping hand', 'share the load', 'have someone's back', 'give someone a leg up', 'save someone's bacon', 'turn a blind eye (if you don't want to help)', 'let someone down'.

Differentiation
Support: Monitor groups as they share ideas and check that everyone has a chance to speak.

Extension: Discuss questions that go beyond the text: *When is it a good idea (or not) to ask for help?*

6. A tight rule

Objective
To prepare and present a speech, speaking audibly and fluently.

What you need
Copies of *The Girl Who Stole an Elephant*, dictionaries and thesauruses, internet access/ encyclopedias for research.

Cross-curricular link
History

What to do

- Read aloud from Chapter 44, modelling expression and fluency. Ask: *What kind of ruler is the King?* (cruel, unreasonable, fearful, heartless, jealous, harsh, unkind, ruthless). Discuss synonyms and antonyms for these adjectives using dictionaries and thesauruses.

- Invite the children to skim the story for examples of how the King speaks and behaves towards the people and how they feel about him. Discuss expressions like 'a tight rule', 'rule with an iron fist' and 'strong-handed' in the context of the story.

- Ask: *What do you think makes a good ruler?* In small groups, ask the children to list the characteristics of a good leader (empathetic, fair, role model, positive, committed).

- Invite the children to identify a good leader – this could be someone in their family, a friend, a public figure or a historical person. The children should prepare a short speech about this person, providing some background, context and examples to show the type of leader they are.

- Revise basic speech structure: 'introduction' to catch the audience's attention; 'body' – the main part, giving two or three points/examples; 'conclusion' summarising the speech's main idea.

- Provide time for children to prepare and practise their speeches before they present them. Encourage them to give each other feedback on pace, expression and intonation.

Differentiation
Support: Children can work in pairs to prepare and present the speech.

Extension: Prepare a speech comparing the King and Leela, giving examples.

Author Q & A

- Use these questions to talk about the author of the book.

Q: Where were you born and where did you grow up?

A:

Q: When did you begin writing and what inspired you?

A:

Q: What age groups do you enjoy writing for?

A:

Q: How many books have you written? Is this your first?

A:

Q: What personal experiences have influenced your stories?

A:

Q: What training and education did you get?

A:

Q: What else do you enjoy apart from writing?

A:

Different but similar

- Compare the characters, their backgrounds and experiences. Identify things that are similar and different. Use examples from the text and add your own ideas.

- Discuss how these differences affect their friendship.

Chaya's character	Nour's character
Jungle experiences	**Desert experiences**
Life in a village	**Life in a villa**

 # Helping hands

- Skim the story to find out who helps whom and why. Make notes and say if the help was appreciated and returned.

Chaya helps… _____

_____

Neel helps… _____

_____

Nour helps… _____

_____

- Discuss these questions and make notes.

1. Why do friends sometimes not ask for help?

_____

_____

2. When do friends usually offer to help?

_____

_____

3. Is help always appreciated? Why?

_____

_____

4. When did you last help someone? How did it work out?

_____

_____

GET WRITING ▶

1. Missing!

> ### Objective
> To use organisational and presentational devices to create a poster.
>
> ### What you need
> Copies of *The Girl Who Stole an Elephant*, Extract 4, photocopiable page 41 'Missing!'
>
> ### Cross-curricular link
> Geography

What to do

- Read Extract 4 using the jump-in reading technique. Ask: *What type of text is it?* (non-fiction, information) *How is it different to the story text?* (formal, factual) Together, highlight the key words and headings.

- Write these words on the board: 'audience', 'purpose', 'language', 'layout'. Recall how they link (every text is written for a specific purpose and audience, which determines the language and layout). Ask: *What is the purpose of this text?* (to inform) *Who is the text written for?* (children) *Describe the language used* (formal, clear, factual, simple) *What organisational features are used?*

- Discuss different ways to present information: poster, brochure, slide show and so on.

- Invite the children to use clues in the story to gather facts and make notes about Ananda the elephant's appearance, habitat, behaviour and activities (Chapters 1, 16 to 19, 26 to 30, 39 to 41).

- Ask children to use photocopiable page 41 'Missing!' to create a missing poster to help the public find Ananda, focusing on purpose, audience, language and layout features.

> ### Differentiation
> **Support:** Mind map the information as a class before the children create their poster.
>
> **Extension:** Children do further research on Sri Lanka and create a holiday poster.

2. Narrative voice

> ### Objective
> To explore and plan narratives from a character's perspective.
>
> ### What you need
> Copies of *The Girl Who Stole an Elephant*.

What to do

- Begin by asking the children to remember the difference between first- and third-person narrative. (First-person narrative uses 'I' and gives the reader insight into the character's thoughts and feelings; third-person narrative uses 'he'/'she'/'they' and tells the story from an outsider's perspective.) Ask: *Can you recall examples of books told in different ways? Which do you prefer?*

- Ask: *Who narrates* The Girl Who Stole an Elephant? (third-person narrator) Ask: *Does this narrator have a different perspective to the characters?* (The narrator tells the story from Chaya's perspective – her thoughts are often written as if in dialogue but not punctuated as such.) *Do you like the narrative style? Does it work well? Why?* Invite discussion.

- Read Chapter 17 together, inviting children to jump in. Ask: *How would it be different if Chaya or Nour told the story? Who would you like to hear telling the story?*

- Invite the children to choose a scene to retell from one of the character's perspectives. They begin by reading the scene, plotting the events, then making notes about how the character feels and thinks.

- Ask them to draft their scene in first-person narrative, including thoughts and feelings of the character who is narrating the story. Afterwards, children swap and proofread each other's work.

> ### Differentiation
> **Support:** Revise first- and third-person narrative with example sentences.
>
> **Extension:** Include dialogue in the scene, revising rules for dialogue.

3. Persuasive dialogue

Objective
To write a dialogue, then proofread for punctuation errors.

What you need
Copies of *The Girl Who Stole an Elephant*.

What to do
- Begin by reading aloud the first part of Chapter 4, inviting children to 'jump in' to show the different characters speaking.

- Come *together and ask: Can a story be told without dialogue?* (yes) *Is dialogue important in this story?* (yes) *Why? How does it add to the story?* (helps describe characters, adds to storyline, provides background information, gives reader insight into how characters feel, and so on).

- Ask the children to recall the rules for writing dialogue. List them on the board, including punctuation features. Point out that sometimes the author includes a reporting clause ('he gasped', 'she exclaimed'), but not always.

- Ask pairs to re-read the first section of Chapter 4, assisting each other with expression. Discuss the persuasive language in the dialogue (for example, 'But I insist'; 'But this one's nicer… And it's also…'). Ask: *How do Neel and Chaya try to persuade Nour not to take the box? How does Nour respond?*

- Invite the children to imagine and create a dialogue of a scene from the story where a character tries to persuade another (for example, Chapter 9: Chaya begs the guard to free Neel; Chapter 47: the children plead with the people to stop following the King; at the end of the story Neel and Nour convince Chaya to stop stealing; in the jungle Nour tries to persuade them to turn back).

- Afterwards, the children proofread and edit their writing to correct spelling and punctuation, and to create authenticity and flow.

Differentiation
Support: Children work in pairs or in small groups to plan and draft the dialogue.

Extension: Children write a 'missing' dialogue to add to another scene from the story.

4. That's the way to do it

Objective
To write a set of instructions for a particular purpose and audience.

What you need
Copies of *The Girl Who Stole an Elephant*, examples of instructions, photocopiable page 42 'That's the way to do it'.

Cross-curricular link
Geography

What to do
- Read the second section of Chapter 19 from 'Look, Nour, look at this' to 'There is *no way* I am doing that.' Invite the children to practise giving oral instructions to Nour on how to get on and off an elephant (including 'how to slide off an elephant's head into a river') using clues from the text.

- Ask: *Where do we come across instructions in everyday life?* (recipes, maps, instruction manuals, board games and so on) Together, make notes on the board recalling features of instructions.

- Read Chapter 22, highlighting Nour's statement 'I wish I knew all this stuff.' Ask: *What does Nour wish she could do? What survival things do the children have to do in the jungle?* (swim, climb a tree, make a fire, catch and cook a fish, deal with leeches)

- Ask small groups to come up with ideas for 'How to survive in the jungle'. Encourage creative and useful ideas and tips that would have made things easier for the children, such as what to take with them.

- Then ask individuals to write instructions using photocopiable page 42 'That's the way to do it', including features from the checklist, before swapping with a partner to proofread.

Differentiation
Support: Write a simple set of instructions for an everyday activity like making a sandwich.

Extension: Children rewrite the instructions as an explanation paragraph.

5. Fire!

Objective
To select appropriate grammar and vocabulary to write a descriptive passage.

What you need
Copies of *The Girl Who Stole an Elephant*, photocopiable page 43 'Fire!', thesauruses.

What to do

- Model reading from Chapter 39 'The fire roared and caught a clump of trees' to the end of Chapter 40.

- Discuss the descriptive language. Ask: *How does the author build tension in the scene?* (powerful images and vocabulary, repetition of the phrase 'fire spreading') *Which words describe the fire and its effects?* (roared, spreading, flared, crackled, burning, smoke drifting, flames snaked, roofs blazed) *Which colours are mentioned?* (auburn glow, waves of scarlet fire) Write responses on the board.

- In small groups, ask children to make a 'fire' mind map of descriptive words and phrases from the text then use thesauruses to find synonyms for these words and make up new descriptive phrases.

- Explore extended metaphors. Consider the image 'flames snaked through the village'. Compare a fire to a snake using appropriate vocabulary. Together, write an extended metaphor on the board. (For example, 'The fire slithered swiftly along, then reared its cruel head, hissing and spitting, flicking its venomous tongue at terrified onlookers!')

- Ask children to use photocopiable page 43 'Fire!' to draft and write their own descriptive passage. Children choose effective and appropriate expressions, vocabulary and grammar to describe the fire. To add to the effect of the descriptive passage, the line 'And the fire kept spreading' is repeated every few lines.

- Children read their descriptions aloud using expression. Display their work for everyone to enjoy.

Differentiation
Support: Using the letters F-I-R-E, write an acrostic poem with words and phrases to describe the fire.

Extension: Write a descriptive passage about the jungle, including an extended metaphor.

6. What if...?

Objective
To write a different ending to the story in the same narrative style and tense.

What you need
Copies of *The Girl Who Stole an Elephant*.

What to do

- Begin by asking: *How do you feel when a story ends? Is the ending always happy or satisfactory? Can you think of examples of when you finished a book and felt sad or dissatisfied or happy?*

- Together, read the final two chapters aloud, inviting readers to 'jump in' as directed. Ask: *What happens in the end?* (the King is overthrown, Queen Leela sets things right, the children are rewarded, families are reunited) *How would you describe the ending?* (happy, satisfactory, positive outcome) *How does the author create a peaceful atmosphere in the final paragraph?* (people chatting and laughing, delicious food cooking, children playing, everyone feels safe and happy, Ananda's trumpeting signifies peace)

- Invite the children to imagine a different outcome to Chapter 47. Ask: *What if the King decided not to step down? What if Leela declared war? What if the villagers turned on Chaya and her friends?* Discuss ideas.

- In small groups, invite the children to plot events that could have occurred to change the story's ending. Include notes on the setting, the atmosphere and how characters feel, speak and behave.

- Individually, children plan and write a different final chapter in the same narrative style and tense as the book. They should include descriptions of the setting, atmosphere and characters, and also add some dialogue. Afterwards, invite the children to read their story endings aloud to the class.

Differentiation
Support: Children rewrite the ending of Chapter 47 in a small group.

Extension: End Chapter 47 with a cliffhanger, suggesting a follow-up book, then ask children to write the introduction to the sequel.

Missing!

- Create a 'missing' poster for Ananda. Include: appearance; likes and dislikes; 'Last seen…' and 'Reward'.

That's the way to do it

- Write a set of instructions and tips for Chaya and her friends on how to survive in the jungle.

How to survive in the jungle	
Equipment:	
What to do to stay safe:	
1.	
2.	
3.	
4.	
5.	
What to do in an emergency:	
Warning:	

Fire!

- Write a descriptive passage about the fire in Chapter 39. Repeat the phrase 'and the fire kept spreading' for effect.

_____

_____

_____

And the fire kept spreading. _____

_____

_____

_____ And the fire kept spreading.

_____

_____

And the fire kept spreading. _____

_____

_____

_____

_____

_____ And the fire kept spreading.

ASSESSMENT ▶

1. Read aloud

> ### Objectives
> To read aloud with expression and meaning; to speak audibly and fluently.
>
> ### What you need
> Copies of *The Girl Who Stole an Elephant*, Extract 3.
>
> ### Cross-curricular link
> Drama

What to do

- Refer to Chapter 1 and invite the children to recall how the story begins (a chase scene). Point out that the story has many chase scenes, where the children flee from danger. Discuss how this adds to the story's adventure and excitement.

- Prepare the children to listen as you read from the story. Read Extract 3 using a boring tone, with many pauses and some errors. Afterwards, ask: *Did you enjoy listening to it? Did its meaning change? What is important when reading aloud?*

- Invite the children to recall important elements of reading aloud and write them on the board: expression, pace, tone, fluency. Discuss how these elements change according to the scene – for example, a chase scene has a fast pace, but a descriptive scene may have a leisurely pace.

- Ask pairs to find another chase scene in the story to read aloud to each other, giving feedback and practising until it sounds fluent and expressive.

- Individually, children then choose any chase scene to read aloud to the teacher, their group or the whole class. Give a rating for each read-aloud element.

> ### Differentiation
> **Support:** Practise reading a short passage using model reading or paired reading.
>
> **Extension:** Read exciting extracts aloud with expression to a large audience to encourage other children to read the book.

2. Read for meaning

> ### Objective
> To understand what they read and answer questions.
>
> ### What you need
> Copies of *The Girl who Stole an Elephant*, photocopiable page 47 'Read for meaning'.

What to do

- Explain that the children will complete a reading task to check their understanding by answering different types of question. Discuss different types of question that could be asked about the book, using examples: recall facts (*What genre is the book? Who pulls Chaya from the river?*); analysis of the text, supported with evidence (*What type of person is Chaya?*); interpretation and opinion, with evidence (*Explain whether you think Chaya's thieving is acceptable*).

- Invite the children to recall tips for reading with understanding. Make notes on the board: first, skim the text for clues on what it's about to get the general context; second, read the text to gather details; third, read the questions to get an idea of the kind of information they need; finally, scan the text again, searching for specific information to answer questions.

- Hand out photocopiable page 47 'Read for meaning'. Read the questions and Chapter 14 together first, reminding learners that the story depicts a fictional time and place. Manage and discuss any responses sensitively, as necessary.

- Ask individuals to complete the comprehension in their notebooks or on a separate sheet.

> ### Differentiation
> **Support:** Read Chapter 14 together as a class using choral or echo reading techniques to build confidence and comprehension.
>
> **Extension:** Add further, higher-order, questions to the ones provided.

3. A letter from the heart

Objective
To write a letter, choosing the appropriate language and register.

What you need
Copies of *The Girl Who Stole an Elephant*.

Cross-curricular link
PSHE

What to do

- Begin by asking the children to recall a time when they received some sort of post (a card or a parcel or even a letter). Ask: *What type of post was it? What was the purpose? How do people prefer to send 'letters' these days and why?* (emails, messages; quicker, more convenient and reliable) Discuss different types of 'letters' (friendship, permission, complaint, demand, invitation).

- Read Chaya's letter to her father in Chapter 18. Ask: *What was the purpose and tone?* (a personal explanation in a familiar tone)

- Discuss how a letter differs from speaking to someone and then discuss and compare formal and informal styles (language, tone, format). For example, in Chapter 48, Chaya shows the guard her invitation from the Queen. Ask: *What language, tone, format would it have had?* (formal, concise, polite)

- Ask the children to recall the format of a letter, making notes on the board (address, greeting, introduction stating the purpose, a paragraph with details, conclusion explaining expected outcome, appropriate sign-off with name).

- Invite the children to plan and write a reply letter from Chaya's father. Consider the tone, the style and how he might have felt at the time. Ask: *What would he say in response to her letter?*

- Individually, children draft a letter then proofread their writing for spelling and punctuation errors.

Differentiation
Support: Children work in groups or pairs to plan and draft the letter, then write it out alone.

Extension: Children choose another scenario and write a letter from one character to another.

4. Hyphenated words

Objective
To use hyphens to avoid ambiguity and enhance their writing.

What you need
Copies of *The Girl Who Stole an Elephant*, dictionaries.

What to do

- Write some hyphenated words on the board (such as 'man-eating', 're-cover', 'twenty-four', 'self-control') and ask the children to identify the common element (hyphen) and recall its purpose (hyphens help link the meaning of words in a concise, unambiguous way).

- Explain the hyphen's different uses and functions: with some prefixes ('ex-', 'self-', 'non-', 're-'), with near homophones ('re-press', 'repress'), to split vowels ('re-enter' is easier to read and understand than 'reenter'), in compound adjectives where two or more words become a single adjective before a noun (four-poster bed), compound nouns ('forget-me-nots', 'half-sister'), numbers from 21 to 99 ('sixty-seven') and fractions ('one-third').

- Remind the children to use hyphens only when necessary; when in doubt, check it out.

- Discuss examples of ambiguity such as 'a light, blue basket' (a blue basket which is not heavy) versus 'a light-blue basket' (a basket in a pale shade of blue). The general rule with compound adjectives is to use a hyphen if the unhyphenated words may be ambiguous.

- Nizrana Farook uses compound adjectives to build descriptions in many scenes. Invite the children to find examples in the story. List hyphenated words from the story on the board.

- Invite the children to draft and write a short paragraph describing a scene in the jungle using at least five compound adjectives.

Differentiation
Support: Practise adding hyphens to compound adjectives.

Extension: List near-homophones such as 're-cover'/'recover'. Children check meanings in dictionaries then write a sentence to show how each word is used.

5. Write and perform

> **Objective**
> To write and perform a scene from the story.
>
> **What you need**
> Copies of *The Girl Who Stole an Elephant*.
>
> **Cross-curricular link**
> Drama

What to do

- Together, read Chapter 21 from 'They walked briskly on' to '"I want to go h-home."' (the leech scene).

- Invite small groups to then briefly act out the 'leech scene' and present their role play to the class. Afterwards, discuss challenges they faced as actors and as the audience. Ask: *Did everyone know what to say? Did everyone have a chance to speak? Could you hear and see everything?*

- Afterwards, discuss ways they could improve their performance. Together, write down some group acting tips on the board: work together, choose a director, speak clearly, face the audience, be expressive, try to sound like your character, stick to the story, use 'imaginary' props, improvise if necessary so the audience is not distracted by 'errors' or miscommunications and so on.

- Invite the children to recall basic script format: title, character names on the left of page, direct speech without speech marks, stage directions in brackets telling characters where to stand and what expression to use.

- In small groups, children then write a script for the whole of Chapter 21, paying attention to correct script format.

- Allow time to practise and present in front of the class. Assess their ability to use their own scripts to perform in front of the class.

> **Differentiation**
>
> **Support:** Limit the scriptwriting to the 'leech scene' then ask children to act it out and compare it to their first attempt.
>
> **Extension:** Children choose any scene from the story, write a detailed script with stage directions (and possibly performance notes) and then perform it.

6. In a nutshell

> **Objective**
> To summarise the story to tell others about it.
>
> **What you need**
> Copies of *The Girl Who Stole an Elephant*.

What to do

- Begin by asking: *Does this story follow a particular pattern or structure?* Invite responses.

- Draw a timeline on the board and mark the beginning and end. Invite the children to recall standard story structure (beginning, problem/challenge, build up, climax, conclusion/resolution). Encourage the children to recall stories they've read or heard that have this structure. Ask: *Can you recall similar stories you've read or watched or heard? What was similar? What was different?*

- Divide the class into groups to plot some of the key events on a timeline and make notes. They should include information about the relevant characters, the setting, the atmosphere and themes in the story.

- Afterwards, invite the groups to share their ideas with the class while other groups add to their notes. Encourage collaboration. Write interesting and useful vocabulary on the board.

- Discuss how to write a story summary: identify the audience and purpose, use the third person, talk about events in chronological order, use the present tense, highlight main events and characters, use your own words, be concise. Provide sentence starters such as: *The story begins in…, The main characters are…, The challenge they face is…, Things become exciting when…, The climax of the story is when…, In the end….*

- Individually, children write a summary of the story. Children then check and edit their work before illustrating it. Display their work on the wall or as a slideshow.

> **Differentiation**
>
> **Support:** Children write one paragraph summarising the plot.
>
> **Extension:** Children write a book review for an online bookshop, summarising the story without giving the ending or twist away, including a personal opinion.

Read for meaning

- Answer these questions about Chapter 14.

1. What problem does Chaya face in the opening paragraph?

2. How does Chaya help Neel escape from his prison cell?

3. Where are the guards taking the children?

4. What distracts the guards?

5. Find two collective nouns that are used to describe the guards.

6. What do these expressions mean in this chapter?

   a. 'The world edged into black.'

   b. 'He's coming to already.'

   c. 'lose your heads'

   d. '*She* was finished.'

7. Explain the effect of italics in the sentence '*What was happening?*'

8. How did the guards treat Chaya and Neel? How would the situation be different today? Explain.

9. Why does Chaya need a 'miracle' and what might it be?

10. Choose a word pair to describe the atmosphere at the beginning and end of this chapter.

    a. chaos – calm

    b. danger – safety

    c. fear – relief

    d. panic – peace

    Then describe how the atmosphere changes.

SCHOLASTIC

READ & RESPOND

Available in this series:

978-1407-15879-2

978-1407-14224-1

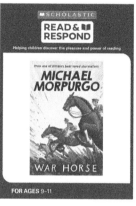

978-1407-16063-4

978-1407-16056-6

978-1407-14228-9

978-1407-16069-6

978-1407-16070-2

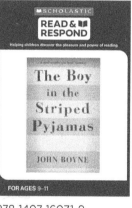

978-1407-16071-9

978-1407-14230-2

978-1407-16057-3

978-1407-16064-1

978-1407-14223-4

978-0702-30890-1

978-0702-30859-8

To find out more,
visit www.scholastic.co.uk/read-and-respond